BINDWEED

BINDWEED

Poems by Leah Johnson

Cherry Grove Collections

© 2021 by Leah Johnson

Published by Cherry Grove Collections
P.O. Box 541106
Cincinnati, OH 45254-1106

ISBN: 9781625493798

Poetry Editor: Kevin Walzer
Business Editor: Lori Jareo

Visit us on the web at www.cherry-grove.com

ACKNOWLEDGEMENTS

My heartfelt thanks to poet David Keplinger—mentor, teacher, friend—and The Surrey Street Poets.

I am grateful to the editors of the following publications in which these poems first appeared:

Beltway Poetry Quarterly: "The Goldfinch"

Green Mountains Review Online: "Meat Locker"

Oberon Poetry: "The Sun Inside"

The Ekphrastic Review: "My Grandfather on a Summer Evening," "One Home"

The Healing Muse: "Dolly," "Golden Rule," "Among Strawberry Vines," "The Last Time," "All Vain Defense," "The Loved Ones"

US Represented: "I Have Been a Stranger to My Garden"

One Art: "Amulet"

For my mother
Aspasia Anastos

Table of Contents

I

These Lenten Days: An Antiphonal Chant   13

Bindweed   14

First Story   15

Blue Summer Evening   16

Butcher   17

The Sun Inside   19

Golden Rule   20

Something Dark Wants to be Known   22

August Corn in New England   23

In a Tongue I Don't Know   24

Maggie's Orchard   25

Love and Hubris   26

Among Strawberry Vines   28

Standing in the Doorway   29

Summer Time With the Brittons, 1962   31

Albums   32

Night Shift   33

II

I Have Been A Stranger to my Garden   37

One Home   39

Waving Her White Handkerchief   41

Each Night   43

My Grandfather on a Summer Evening   44

Eclipse   46

At the Edge of Spring   47

The Loved Ones   48

Coal   49

My Mother Disappeared in October   50

Meat Locker   52

Green   53

Uncle Billy   54

Dolly   56

February   58

III

The White Pigeon   63

Learning to See at Kettle's Yard   67

The Last Time   69

Communion   71

The Blue Moon Snail at Brewster Flats   73

Old Friend   74

Song   76

Bright Secular Day   79

Reconfigurations   80

I'm Not There Anymore   81

My Mother Loved My Hands   83

Last Leaf on the Oak   84

All Vain Defense   85

My Deaths   86

The Goldfinch   89

Amulet   90

About the Author   91

I.

THESE LENTEN DAYS: AN ANTIPHONAL CHANT

I always weep when I think of Easter
for the darkness that precedes Easter.

For the inky Lenten days of denial and toil
as I trudge towards Easter.

For my grandparents weaning themselves from sin, determined and loyal
fasting for the forty days before Easter.

For the priest's thumb tracing the cross on my forehead with warm oil
in the house of incense four days before Easter.

For my child-self on Holy Friday morning crawling into the flowered tomb of dark
  soil
to kiss the icon of Christ who will rise on Easter.

And shall I not rise, shall we all not rise with him, released from the mire of these
  Lenten days?
Shall we not all sing *Christos Anesti,* Christ has risen?

BINDWEED

On my knees in the morning grass I reach
for the bindweed strangling you
slide my fingers down
its smooth sturdy stem, follow
to where it meets the soil.

I tug, pull it out, knowing
once again I've failed
to source its root. It will return.

Patience darling, as I carefully unwind
from your stem, your leaves, your bud.
Release your young body.

FIRST STORY

God is in every particle of everything.
I tucked this gift into a little pocket
in my heart. I was so happy through morning
ablutions, making the bed, eating breakfast,
sweeping the front porch, watering the plants.
I was loving the heck out of every particle
of everything. My mind began to parse.
Even in the concrete the workmen next door
are pouring onto the walkway? The plastic
bags hanging on the doorknob for recycling?
The plastic straws killing sea turtles? The atom bomb?
Even in my friend's lymphoma? In the
chemotherapy ravaging her body?
How can Mystery not discriminate?
And can Spirit be in all these things and still
reside elsewhere as well, like having
a vacation house in the Bahamas and
an apartment in New York City? I could
have gone on like this all day. I could have gone on
dissecting, like peeling an orange and pulling
its segments apart. Or the mad act
of cutting into an apple, and eating it.

BLUE SUMMER EVENING

She sees herself on a blue summer evening,
arms flung out, spinning round as she
stares up at the darkening sky, loses her
balance and falls to the cool grass, dizzy with freedom.
And she sees all the things that aren't in this picture:
the enormous backyard, trailing like the wake
of the great grey ship of their two-family
house, and floating in that wake the small wooden
sandbox where she filled her cousin's ears and
nostrils with damp yellow sand. Grapevines
along the back fence, her child-self— impatient
for the taste of grape—polishing a hard green
berry on her sundress, biting into it,
surprised and delighted by crunch and sour.
And later, squeezing ripe Concord grapes out of
their purple-black skins into her mouth,
spitting hard seeds, savoring the taste of sweet,
the feel of it sliding down her throat.

BUTCHER

Those summer days I sat
all elbows and knees
on the worn wooden steps
of the corner store.

Sucking my Popsicle,
excavating a Dixie Cup
with a flat wooden spoon, chewing
red wax lips, Bazooka gum,
Good and Plenty.

Nights I sleepwalked my way
through my childhood, dreamed
I was a spinning top stuck
in the spinning spot watching
the hands of the kitchen clock
circling crazily backwards.

Some days I returned
soda bottles for a nickel each,

picked up fresh hamburg
for dinner, watched him shove
the cold raw beef
into the grinder.

THE SUN INSIDE

Early mornings the stepsister of dread inhabits my body
and pins me to the bed.
Even though salt air rushes in through screens and stings
my nostrils, wraps me in its damp arms.
Even though dune grasses dance behind my eyelids
and I wake with the sea in my mouth.

*

Autumn 1968, Syracuse. I was tripping on mescaline
and Jeannie was rose and gold and chestnuts.
Sitting on an old sofa on the roof of Lehman Hall in winter
wrapped in blankets
I peeled an orange and handed out the segments
one at a time.

*

Because we loved the Beatles,
because we made love not war.
And the ancient empty street's too dead for dreaming
hadn't yet become our anthem.
Because on the red pillow of passion I lay my head each night
and each morning woke sober.
Because I rolled up the hill of Crouse College in the spring grass.

GOLDEN RULE

On his bed of dry ice
my father lay still and silent,
window cracked open.

We bathed him
Biblically
in lavender water

laid him out,
dressed him,
tugging his grey slacks

over bent knees,
buttoning his
blue shirt.

He had painted
his entire house
when he was eighty,

raked fifteen bags
of leaves from my yard,
cleaned my basement,

scrubbed and waxed my car,
clipped coupons,
packed my groceries,

washed my dishes,
watched my children
every New Year's Eve.

I had one chance
to get this right.
And I did.

SOMETHING DARK WANTS TO BE KNOWN

Before I hear it roar, before I turn
to see it rush towards me, I feel
the sleep tsunami quake:
My lips disappear.
My mouth fills with ice.
My husband lies on the bed
dead, zombie eyes wide-opened,
a bald man with a round face
next to him alive and grinning.
Who the hell are you?
I hear my words distorted
cross the room in slow motion
like a record on the wrong speed.
Pushing against the walls
of my body-cave, something dark.
A wild white stallion
at the bedroom window
tears the screen, shatters
the glass with his hooves;
I can do nothing.

AUGUST CORN IN NEW ENGLAND

In your sheaths how
like you to hide
your ripening from us.
So still and demure
in your seasonal procession,
row on row wrapped
tightly. Everything
around you throbs, heaves
and swells, pushes against
the boundaries of form.
To be born to something new
is to be charged with holiness.

IN A TONGUE I DON'T KNOW

Six, eight, nine, ten, twelve

years old, and angry words fast fly round the room

in a tongue I don't know, yet have heard all my life.

Dear tongue turned hot and cruel. Words bounce off walls,

veer right and left. Mute, deaf, I feel each jab,

shot, stab, blast not aimed at me,

each piece of shrapnel lodge in my chest. This time

I see your old lined face, see you're caught too.

As they go on with hurl and roar I lay you

down, pull up the old gold throw,

stroke your brow, your veined hand, sing you

to sleep in a tongue I don't know,

yet have heard all my life.

MAGGIE'S ORCHARD

Turn around and turn left
up the first dirt road, past
the peeling barns of the

artist studios, broad red
and grey brush strokes in a
fading green landscape.

When you reach the apple
orchard, you've arrived.
In last spring's winds,

the haughty trees tossed their
white-blossomed hair against
the blue skies. Now their

humbled brown limbs are heavy
with apple, waiting for us
to come, relieve them of their burden.

LOVE AND HUBRIS

My mother and I sat on the terrace of Les Deux Magots
holding hands, her silver hair coiffed.
But I was young and beautiful
in my Rodier linen shirt and sunglasses.
And I spoke French.

We sat cross-legged on the bed in our
tiny room on Rue Ferdinand, breakfasted
on croissants and drank from tall thin glasses
our knees touching. In the Jeu de Paume, she fell
in love with the Monets and couldn't stop talking about them.

We strolled in the shade of plane trees down
a deserted street on Ile Saint-Louis
to a restaurant I'd discovered, and for once
enjoyed a Sunday dinner she hadn't had to cook herself.
Then she asked for American coffee.

American coffee, I thought, and turned my head away.
I think of Persephone whose mother roamed
and searched the lonely earth for her.
The weight of her grief an anvil

on her back, her daughter in Hades eating
the three seeds.

AMONG STRAWBERRY VINES

Among strawberry vines, the sun
baking my back, I reached for the ripe
heart-shapes, popped them into my mouth.
The entire yard was covered, a bright red
jubilee. It looked and tasted like
healing. But lying here in the dark,
remembering how he climbed onto
my small body, I choke on the tangled
strawberry vines, clinging to earth.

STANDING IN THE DOORWAY

Blood of the Sunday roast pooled on the platter, blood
of the skinned knees and scraped elbows, blood

of the spear-shaped cut on my brother's temple pouring down his face—
Blood of Christ in the gold chalice, blood

in the tiny silver spoon brought to my mouth—
Blood of the razor's nick on my father's chin, blood

of the needle's prick on my arm—
of my other brother's black eye, a purple storm beneath the skin, blood

of the tonsillectomy spewed into the chrome pan—
of my mother's first menstruation when she thought she was dying, blood

of my first menstruation arrived at last—
Blood every month. Every month blood.

When we were fourteen, Diana Peck pulled me into her bedroom,
whispered, "My mother is crying because she lost her baby

yesterday. She sat on the toilet, and it dropped
into the water. She flushed it away." Oh,

how could I understand such loss? How could I
know that death stands in the doorway next to life?

SUMMER TIME WITH THE BRITTONS, 1962

Round and round the house
he shuffled in his baggy brown pants
and greying tee shirt, groaning
or letting loose a blast of profanity.

Mr. Britton was the only rider
on a gruesome carousel, wandering
from room to gloomy room hunched over
clutching a hot water bottle to his side.

The kitchen was the first room
in the house to die. I hated
having to come in
the back door through its brittle casing.

ALBUMS

B is for Beatles
For the afternoons of spinning around
the living room with my friend Sandy
holding hands, singing every word of every lyric of
every song on *Rubber Soul*, collapsing
on the carpet.

For the poster of John in his wire-rim glasses
hanging on the dorm room wall
of my new lover who promises,
"we will be like oil and water"
but holds my hand at the movies instead,
offers me my first joint.

For that morning in Boston riding
in the convertible of a one-night stand
a brilliant September day
and the sun is warming my jeans
and "Come Together" on the radio and I
can't wait to get away.

NIGHT SHIFT

I stand on the back porch
in the wakeful hours, the wandering
hours, and look down

at my lavender, my thyme
still and silent in their bed, breathing
without a sound, tucked in for the night

in the lambent moonlight. But they
will not sleep; rhythmic bursts of growth
will drive them, night-stems reaching

farthest just before dawn when
the gate will close. I am
reminded of my own nights:

the locked white door in the corner store
the grinning bald man in the coffin, eyes open
me standing alone in the living room, bleeding

calling for help, and the reach for meaning
as on a scrap of paper
I write your name.

II.

I HAVE BEEN A STRANGER TO MY GARDEN

I peer out the sunroom window
at the hydrangeas encroaching
on the arborvitaes, the camellia —
and just now in mid-November when
the tight buds of the camellia are grasping
at every bit of waning sun
to bloom and the arborvitaes
are struggling to spread their branches.
They can't do this by themselves.
But how can I disturb the oak leaf in its
massive burgundy glory? The *paniculata*
with its fragile dried blossoms intact?
The camellia has become deformed
leaning to the left, withered on the right
like a paralytic. On my hands and knees
I survey the lower branches
of the arborvitaes, crush the brittle leaves.
Death creeping from the bottom up.
(I hadn't known it was this bad.)
Like a stranger, I slay the *paniculata*
to a bundle of sticks, attack the oak leaf
from the rear, leaving only its two

front branches on fire in the sunlight.

Limbs are scattered all over

the lawn. I survey my work and see

that it is without grace, that I have maimed

in my haste to release the captives. And I pray

for my soul's return in the slow and steady work.

ONE HOME
after William Stafford

Mine was a Greek home—transplanted in New England.
We took root there but rejected its cold code.
From the back porch, we could see
the gold dome of the Orthodox church.

The mingled scent of mothballs, parsley, gardenias—
The whirr of the sewing machine birthing flurries of aprons—
The braided *kouloudia* and sugar-dusted *kourabiedes* in red and gold tins—
The bottle of home-made brandy under the kitchen sink—

The stark white enamel stove was GE, electric;
lemon-oregano chicken sizzled in the oven.
Outside, peaches and quinces and currants—
and the sun reflected in a mercury ball.

My grandfather fingered his amber worry beads:
"Marry a Greek or marry a Jew, but
whatever you do, don't marry a Yankee."
(We took root there but rejected their cold code.)

On hot summer days, my cousins and I roamed the streets
of the old factory town where nothing ever happened
dragged back home to jump on the beds
and eat bowls of fresh peaches with whipped cream.

WAVING HER WHITE HANDKERCHIEF

Us, around the kitchen table,
roast in the oven, shot glasses
sparkling *Metaxa*—I hang on
every incomprehensible
word, ride the rhythms and resonance,
sense the shifts when tension
through the seams of their talk
stitches like thread on *YiaYia's* machine.

After dinner, I make *PaPou* his coffee,
as he has taught me, in the battered
brass *briki*, carefully balance
the white and gold porcelain demitasse
of foamy dark liquid on its saucer,
offer it to him as he sits
in the big chair by the fireplace
having a smoke.

Sometimes *YiaYia* dances, a heavy
old woman with the step of a schoolgirl
weaving her way through the living room

to the pierce and pluck
of clarinet and bouzouki,
waving her white handkerchief,
reaching out to me, and we whirl
to "*opa's*" and "*yasou's.*"

When *PaPou* lies on the sofa,
I cover him with the afghan
YiaYia knit for me, row upon row
the colors of corn, of wheat, of sunflowers.
My grandfather with the heart of a farmer,
who has worked in the shoe factories all his life,
lies napping in a golden field.

EACH NIGHT

Each night the pillow
of fear. Each night a small death.
And my body still
my mind's captive.

MY GRANDFATHER ON A SUMMER EVENING
after Mark Strand

When the summer sun slants
towards the horizon, casts its eerie light,
the shadows of the peach and quince trees lengthen
on the grass, the Rose of Sharon glows stark white.
My grandfather, a cigarette between his thumb and forefinger,
a glass of brandy on the table by his side
sits on the porch and looks down upon his small domain
his reward for hours days weeks months years
spent in the dark of the shoe factory
stretching pieces of leather over wooden forms.

Soon the red-hot cinder of my grandfather's cigarette
the cold flickering light of the fireflies
will dot the darkness, and still he will sit,
ponder the marvels of Ancient Greece,
Alexander who hailed from his own small piece
of that great territory, ponder, as if thinking could protect him.

My grandfather will come indoors,
his thoughts will come with him,
as the fruit trees, the shrubs, the currant
and the blueberry, dig their roots in deeper,

in his garden the corn stalks grow silk

tomatoes turn from green to red.

He will settle into his dark oak Morris chair

drape his arms over the carved lions' heads.

Then he will look up, notice me

sitting in front of him on the Turkish leather cushion.

He'll lean forward, our knees touching now, take my hands in his:

"There is only one God, and He loves everyone

no matter how small."

ECLIPSE

I started drawing circles to contain
myself, to keep from bleeding
out. The bright yellow circle
of my childhood stained
with black ink. The grey-green circle
of despair. Lightning bolts of panic
zig-zagging across a pale blue disc.
And when you were away —
the black sphere of fear bearing down
on me, swallowing my sleep.

AT THE EDGE OF SPRING

Purple heads of crocus push up through soil
through grass, deep green spears of daffodils
buds in translucent sheaths, a drift of snowdrops,
yellow hellebores beneath a grey
dogwood tree.

You will not return.
Calls of robin, cardinal, crow—grey wing,
red wing, black wing, worms and bits of twine
dangle from beaks. "In springtime, in springtime,
the only pretty ring time" runs through my head and
"You will not return, not return, not…."

I bundle babies
into the buggy, fat fists and chubby cheeks,
push off for the park.
Raise my face to the sun.

THE LOVED ONES

They feel so heavy, these
pressing upon my heart, crowding my lungs.
Sometimes, I can barely breathe.
I feed them on bits of longing and regret.
Keep them alive to give birth to them again
and again. It is a dark and desperate nurturing.
Yet I fear to cut the black cord.
Will they float away as my old lover did?
Suppose I were to feed them on
sips of moonlight. Wing-hovering air.
The hummingbird's beak dipping into
columbine? Feed them on drops of dew
resting in grass, refulgent in sunlight.
I am unaccustomed to lightness.

COAL

I remember it
being poured through our
cellar window. Huge black
pile like death itself, indelible,
smudging our small hands.
But I was speaking of a raven.
It soars, it overbears, it perches
on the branches of gum trees
and palms, dark omen from
the Middle Ages, for this time.
But its call surprises all the fear
out of me. Bumping down
the steps of the scale
like a clumsy child,
fa–mi–re, it lands on *do*
with a mournful little wail,
a shy complaint. I picture a tiny
infant mourner or a toothless crone.
How unlike the coal. How
unlike the terrifying crow
with its insistent monotone.

MY MOTHER DISAPPEARED IN OCTOBER

Leaves flashed gold orange crimson, lit up
the hills north of Boston into New Hampshire, Maine,
Vermont. Great swathes of glorious color. On the cool ground,
squirrels hoarded nuts for winter. Travelers headed home
after the long weekend; lines of cars sped
the black and white highways. It was a sunny day.

Far from New England, rain poured down, drowned out
the sounds of travelers' goodbyes, whispered and otherwise.
Trees still verdant except the dogwoods hinting at
an early red, leaves dripping. Government offices were closed.
Workers slept in or cradled cups of coffee in their hands.
Sat by windows and watched the ruining rain.

Sheets of grey-blue rain beat down on black tarmac, pelted
cars and trucks speeding along the highways.
North, a sudden stop in the blinding rain and
an eighteen wheeler smashed into them from the rear.
She blew through the windshield and flew away.
This is the picture the psychic drew, an angel flying out of a car;
he didn't draw her landing on the hard tarmac. In the rain.

The doctor sat on his side of the desk. *Brain impact*, he said.
Vegetable. Hopeless. Machines. Children home from school
sat sprawled in front of TV's in their pajamas, dipped
triangles of toast into hot chocolate. The hospital
cold blue light and electronic sounds. The psychic drew
a figure of a woman on a narrow cot, alone.

MEAT LOCKER

Where the devil is a butcher
in a white apron
smeared with red.

I am a bloody slab
hanging on a hook.
"You tell anyone, I'll

kill you," he whispers,
and my terror cleaves me in two,
my body

on its hands and knees
in that cold with the butcher,
my mind a white balloon.

GREEN

A hard sound for so many soft things:
mosses, grasses, sages, mints, ferns, laurels,
pines, clovers, leaves of all kinds. It comes from

the Old English *grene* or the Northumbrian *groene*,
the Old Saxon *grani*, Old Frisian *grene*, Dutch *groen*
Old Norse *groenn*, Old High German *gruoni*. How did

the touch of grass brushing an ankle, or a leaf
sweeping against a forearm translate to that sound
lodged in the throat? Had they carried it there

from the labors of their daily round? In time,
the English brought it up to the back of the tongue
where it settled and hardened. The French had it

right: going back to the Latin *viridis* and softening
it further to *vert*, a word barely there, a whisper or
a single blade of grass.

UNCLE BILLY

I had forgotten that tiny apartment
my grandmother lived in after my grandfather died.
The steep narrow steps, her ample body perched
at the top, like a bird stuffed into a cage.

I notice him next to her. He has been missing
for decades. Now here he is with his grey-black hair,
his hook nose. I remember the face, younger,
remember the rancor it earned.

Summer 1953. Walking down Prospect Street
on a Saturday afternoon, my six-year old hand in his.
Godzilla and popcorn and Uncle Billy
sitting next to me in the dark, silent as a rook.

Now a sneer visits his face
as he greets me, seeming to delight
in my confusion. Laying claim
to my grandmother as *his*.

He had been christened *Basileus*, meaning king.
And I suppose he was, in his way. He ruled

our lives with his absence, spawning quandary
and conflict, slammed doors and stand-offs.

Uncle Billy established his kingdom
by creating a vacuum, and my grandparents
leapt into that nothingness like mourners
jumping into an open grave.

DOLLY

I don't remember a voice, only
his shadow in the doorway
terrible and familiar
as I shrank to the size of a clothespin doll.

His shadow in the doorway
"*Dolly-mou*" they laughed as they pinched my cheeks
and I shrank to the size of a clothespin doll
among the needlework and the heavy black coffee.

Pinched my cheeks on Sunday afternoons, on the *piazza*, laughing
I slid the bright orange blossoms of trumpet vine over my fingers
among the needlework and the heavy black coffee.
My godfather's arm reached out like a tentacle and pulled me onto his lap.

I slid the bright orange blossoms of trumpet vine over my fingers
the day unwinding like a spool of thread
my Godfather's arm reaching out like a tentacle to pull me onto his lap
his hand sweaty and swollen.

The day unwinding like a spool of thread

terrible and familiar

his hand sweaty and swollen

I don't remember a voice.

FEBRUARY

I sit by the fire
he laid with twigs gathered
    on our walks
from fallen trees, logs
he rolled home and split to keep
    his summer wife warm.

Pen and ink days
bare black branches
    scratch at white sky and I
miss the lemon sunset the
long shadows of trees
    at twilight.

The front door whistles
its ugly music
    in the wind
shuts me in and I miss
the sea and salt
    of my body.

We were married in July.

The candles dripped wax.

    Rivulets of sweat

trickled between my breasts

ran down my belly

    dampened my thighs.

III.

THE WHITE PIGEON

Outside the Masters' Cottage at St. John's, the sidewalk
is strewn with brass daisies
pressed into the stones;
follow those daisies to
the ice-cream cart and around the corner past Trinity,
to a row of Tudor-beamed shops leaded windows
white plaster walls.
St. Mary's tower on the left, the climb up that twisted narrow
staircase is harrowing:
The heavy stone walls
close in the higher you climb, the stone stairs hollowed
beneath your feet.
The only light ekes
in through slits in the walls
like half-opened eyes.

But then the deep breath of release as you stoop and step
out onto the roof, the whole
of the city open before you
under a grey sky, wind blowing

like crazy, a gaggle of school-children
running around, a bearded man leaning
over the edge taking photos.

Down below, the bustle
of Auntie's Tea Shop is palpable
through its plate glass window.
Girls in black skirts and frilly white aprons
scurry from table to kitchen and back
with scones and cream and jam
cress and egg sandwiches on white bread or brown
pots of Darjeeling, Green, Lapsang Souchang,
Black Currant, Chamomile.
The door opens and closes with blasts
of cold air as patrons huddle
in their sweaters and scarves.

A few hardy souls
sit at tables outside
in the shadow of St. Mary's
cupping hot chocolate or tea
in their cold hands
taking in the view of King's College

its expanse of velvet lawn, stripes
of alternating greens.
Two ancient chestnuts vie
with the soaring towers,
spreading their immense branches, coral
blossoms almost spent waiting to fall
and that crazy jester fellow
in his red velvet coat and
floppy hat is pestering tourists sitting on
the wall waiting for evensong.

The stout red-faced beadle in his
white collar and purple robe stands
outside the carved wooden doors
nods as worshippers line up
for the five-thirty service.
Henry the Eighth, similarly stout but
imperious in his armor and sword
looks down on the scene
from his alcove. A white pigeon
perched on his hat shows
no signs of leaving. An hour later

the beadle comes bursting

into the Chophouse headed for the bar.

The pigeon is still there

at home on a king's head.

LEARNING TO SEE AT KETTLE'S YARD

"I am still so bewildered by the beauty of everything here."
That's what Jim Ede said, she told me, as she took my coat,
hung it in the tiny closet, and handed me a small white ticket
with a number scribbled on it. She tucked its twin in the pocket
of my coat and led me into the sitting room.

You can sit on any of the chairs in this house
and that is a remarkable thing, I think—
to be able to sit on a hundred-year-old chair.
This one has just been re-caned and dates back
to the 1800's, and that one is a sixteenth century
great armchair from "the mad grandeur of the Spanish soul."

Everything here is simple and orderly, space
and light and shadow, just as he created it.
See how this bay window lets in the Eastern light,
how it falls on the round beach pebbles he arranged
in an unwinding concentric circle large to small
on this round scrubbed pine table.

And the shadow pattern of the blinds
on the table itself — and that spark of light

on the blue glass ball resting there so quietly.
Resting there so quietly, as does the single lemon
on the pewter tray on that distressed oak trunk.
Nothing else is needed.

He had such an eye for the potential in everyday objects—
for example, notice how this lovely piece twists
up and up until the top where he's placed
those two pressed glass decanters. Would you believe
it's a cider screw he bought for one pound
from two elderly English women who had spent
most of their lives in Normandy?

He never had much money. But he knew beauty.
This fireplace shelf he built with ancient tiles
he found in the neighborhood, and on it
he placed simple, natural items like these two scallop shells
you see reflected in the luster jug behind them.
"My fascination with details will, I hope, never cease.
Each object is a miracle." Jim Ede said that, she told me,
as she pointed out the single feather, grey, in a crystal goblet.

THE LAST TIME

I rise in the night as I do these years
glance out the window
to where the ginkgo tree glows
like a ghost sun.

Each night it catches me
this bright companion
in the autumn dark.

And I ponder its particular beauty,
when it will end:

Which morning will I find the yellow below
and bare grey branches above?
Will its leaves fall all at once
or let go one by one throughout the night?

It's like having children; you never know
the last time
they'll ask to be held as they fall asleep
or take your hand as you cross the street.

They let go without noticing.
And if you stay awake for years
you won't catch
the transmutation.

COMMUNION

When winter severs
the mother cord,
I grow hungry. I sit

at the long table
and slowly, from sheets
of yellow beeswax,

roll candles. The air
becomes hive-haunted,
fills with the warm

hum of bees. Where
do they come from, these
tiny ancient gods?

What is the price
of their visitation? I
light a candle.

Into a jar of amber

I dip the spoon and bring it

to my lips.

THE BLUE MOON SNAIL AT BREWSTER FLATS

My palm longs to hold its full moon
blue and cool, its great foot pulsing, this
survivor from the Triassic Era. It is not
ploughing through the sand in relentless search
of prey, is not hauling and enveloping and boring;
its sandpaper tongue is not scraping and devouring.
This low tide is its Sabbath tide, a respite from
the work of surviving for 252 million years. A time
to be held in beauty as beauty—singular, compressed.

OLD FRIEND
for Chip Harding

I was hanging on
by the threads of music and friendship
as we sat at the table in your January kitchen
the Maine snow falling in pie-sized flakes.

The threads of music and friendship
wove us together
the Maine snow falling in pie-sized flakes
our voices rising.

Wove us together
first in the New Hampshire woods
where our voices rose
as we talked and you sang our way through the dark.

In the New Hampshire woods
you with your guitar and your gift
we talked and you sang our way through the dark
the stillness around us a green veil.

You with your guitar and your gift
as we sat at the table in your January kitchen
the stillness around us a silver veil—
and I was hanging on.

SONG

Scarlatti, Rossini, Verdi
sonata, opera, aria
pianissimo, fortissimo

andante, adagio, allegro
moderato, lento, presto—
sotto voce.

If you press
the narrow wooden key
of the clavichord,

the tangent strikes a string
brass or iron–
a barely audible sound.

Vibrate the key with your finger;
the string too vibrates
with a breathless whisper.

The harpsichord is another story:
Plectra of crow quill or leather
pluck the metal strings

when you depress the keys
you feel the slightest
delight of resistance.

All sparkle
and resonance as the choirs
of strings sing out *forte*.

In 1700 Bartolomeo Cristofori
(the name itself sings)
of Padua, Italy enters the scene

with his *fortepiano*
which marries the expressive clavichord
with the resonant harpsichord.

Neither pressing nor plucking
the hammers of the *fortepiano*
hit the metal strings.

To believe this:
The force with which
the fingers hit the keys

dictates the force with which
the hammers hit the strings
all the way
from *pianissimo* to *fortissimo*.

BRIGHT SECULAR DAY

We were taught to speak English, as Greek hovered
all around us, at once familiar and incomprehensible,
in the voices of family and family friends. We ate hamburgers
and french fries, *taramousalata* and *keftedes,* tuna sandwiches
on Pepperidge Farm white bread and *spanakopita*, roast beef
and mashed potatoes, roast lamb and *pilaf,* apple pie and ice cream
and *baklava* dripping with honey. We celebrated Thanksgiving
and American Christmas, Greek Easter and my father's name day.
When we moved, the priest came to bless our house, sprinkling
holy water and waving his thurible, from which clouds of incense
swirled. Sunday mornings I listened to the top forty on the car radio
as my father drove us to church where I climbed the sighing wooden
stairs, crossed myself, kissed the icon and placed the lit candle
in the holy bed of sand, sat for an hour and a half in the near dark
as the Karras brothers' off-key nasal chants and the priest's
haunting "*Kyrie eleisons*" alternately assaulted and soothed
my ears. Rising to leave, I shuffled behind my father, worked
my way to the front of the church, kissed the priest's veined hand
nibbled on my square of white bread, retreated up the center aisle
down the steps and out into the bright secular day where I
hopped into the front seat of the car and turned up the volume
to catch the final top five.

RECONFIGURATIONS

In the mountains, a ramshackle house:
just a large kitchen and a bedroom.
The windowpane next to the bed
is broken, the window inhabited
by a radiant blue hen, fat as a dowager.

My own house appears, transformed
transgressed, not my house at all
though I still know it. I like to return
to certain houses, the one in New England—
simple brown clapboard, no shutters, windows
opened wide—though I've never been inside.

What are these houses,
night after night, year after year?
What are my longings, my body
repeatedly reconfigured? Why
am I still looking?

I'M NOT THERE ANYMORE

A sparrow's nest
is nestled in the boxwood
by the back gate
behind the bird bath.
The two eggs are tiny
speckled with brown–
I wonder
if the mother will return.

Every morning I wash out
the bird bath, refill it
with fresh water–
later, if I'm lucky, I
catch a glimpse of
a robin frolicking in there
like a little kid
in a wading pool
on a hot summer's day.

We have a new front porch.
I sit from afternoon
to early evening, listening

to the birds, their chorus
a wonder of antiphonal sound
as they sing their hearts out.

My body can't sing
with this pillow of dread
stuffed down my throat
filling me
from crotch to neck
keeping me on the dull edge
of nausea.

My body can't sing
with these currents of fear
coursing down my arms
to my hands, my legs
to my feet that want to run
but can't.

I plod up the stairs, open
the box from before
take out the small red sneakers
hold them close and tell myself,
"I'm not there anymore."

MY MOTHER LOVED MY HANDS

"They're so small, where did they come from?"
she marvelled, not quite believing she had made them.
Hers were square and sturdy, strong, served her well
in the surgery where she handed the shiny instruments
to the doctors, where she could have been a surgeon herself.

Served her well as she tended the burn victims from the war
applied ointment, wrapped gauze around their raw
open wounds. Served her well as she wiped the brows
of the shell-shocked boys and men with terror in their eyes.
Mine played the piano. Glided over the satin keys.
This too she found miraculous.

LAST LEAF ON THE OAK

Leaf that was green hasn't
forgotten its greenness.
I watched this morning from the
window, it twisting
in the gale. Clinging.
What will it take to loosen
its grip? This memory-
keeper. This body.

ALL VAIN DEFENSE

The talk had been of age and illness, fear
and death. Awake in the velvet dark, I sensed
a crack in the thin veneer of my soul
even Beauty cannot mend. Even as
the crimson tulip, magnificent in its ruin,
unfurls its satin petals, reveals the black
within. Even as the sage sprawls easy
in the sun, celadon leaves and purple blooms,
savory and sweet. Even as the crape myrtle
bids my hand stroke its silken bark.
All vain defense. Polish me hard, dear God.
Hard as the chestnut. Hard as the beach-white stone.

MY DEATHS

I.
The first time, they pushed me
Down the white linoleum hall
In a square-wheeled wooden gurney
Bumpety-bump, bumpety-bump
Placed the mask over my face
And held it there

The second time, he mounted me
(I shrank to the size of a clothespin doll)
And taught me the daddy game
Humpety-hump, humpety-hump
I placed the mask over my face
And held it there

He locked me, the third time,
In the bright cold of the dead animal stall
Prodded me onto my hands and knees
Rumpety-rump, rumpety-rump
The mask tight to my face
I held it there

The fourth time I died, I awoke

To my other deaths, heard them call

They pulled me down

Bumpety-bump, humpety-hump, rumpety-rump

Tore the mask from my face

Held it away from me

II.

A different death:

    the death of vermillion swathes

the death of the labyrinth walk

    the death of the morning moon

the death of numinous whispers

    the death of swimming in the dark pool of my lover's mouth

the death of galloping clouds

    the death of hot diamonds

the death of lambent light

    the death of bleached bone

the death of sap rushing from roots to trunk

    the death of rampant divinity

III.

We are borne upon the wave

of darkness fierce and simmering.

Survivor, predator,

we are borne upon the wave.

Images float and bob like buoys.

The green sea is roiling.

We are borne upon the wave,

our darkness fierce and simmering.

*THE GOLDFINCH
for David Keplinger

It's about intrigue and injury and losing one's way.
But mostly it's about how beauty sustains us
how in the night we think about it
wrapped up and stashed under our bed
how we can get down on our knees
peer into the dark and retrieve it
untie the twine that binds it, release it
from the layers of fading newspaper
bring it out — ours. Or how
even the belief that we own it
keeps us alive. This
is what you teach us.

* after Donna Tartt's novel, *The Goldfinch*

AMULET

Finally, what do you hold dear?
The calm and quiet of green.
I wear it as an amulet. In these
clamorous times, a hum, a whisper.
A bed laid down amidst the roar.
I want no other song, no other
resting place. Green knows
my nature and my name.

About the Author

Leah Johnson is a Washington, DC poet. A member of the Surrey Street Poets, her work has been published in several journals, including *Green Mountains Review Online, The Healing Muse, Oberon Poetry Magazine, The Aurorean,* and the anthology *Such Friends As These.* She is a 2017 Best of the Net nominee for her poem "The Goldfinch" in *Beltway Poetry Quarterly.* She is a co-host of the WordWorks Café Muse Literary Salon. A Professor Emeritus in Writing Studies at American University, she has also taught piano and co-founded, with Connie Zimmer, Dumbarton Concerts,, now in its 43rd season.

✲ ✲ ✲ ✲ ✲ ✲

Made in the USA
Monee, IL
16 November 2021